KATYD

Pictures & Fun Facts on Animals For Kids

PUBLISHED BY:

Tanya Turner
Copyright © 2017

All rights reserved.

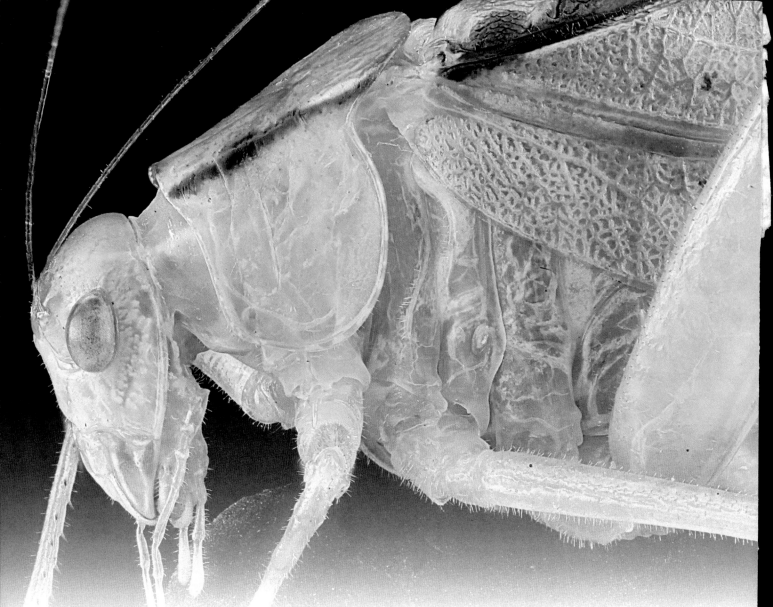

The katydid is a very interesting and cool creature that you can hear outside in the summer.

It is related to crickets and grasshoppers but what's make them different from crickets and grasshoppers is the distinct noise that it makes.

The male katydid creates a very loud call to attract female katydid. The males produce this noise by rubbing their forewings together. In some species of katydid, the female katydid can also make this sound.

Are you ready to learn more fascinating information about the katydid? "Katydid:Pictures & Fun Facts on Animals For Kids " is a wonderfully written book with cute katydid pictures for your kids to discover more about this interesting insect.

Have a copy of this book now and enjoy learning about the katydid!

The katydid is a very long insect with long and skinny antennae, and you could see them jumping around at night.

The Katydids are medium to large-sized insects with thin long legs. Their hind legs which they used for jumping are longer than the front or middle legs.

Microcentrum rhombifolium is the scientific name of the Katydid.

Where can you find katydids?

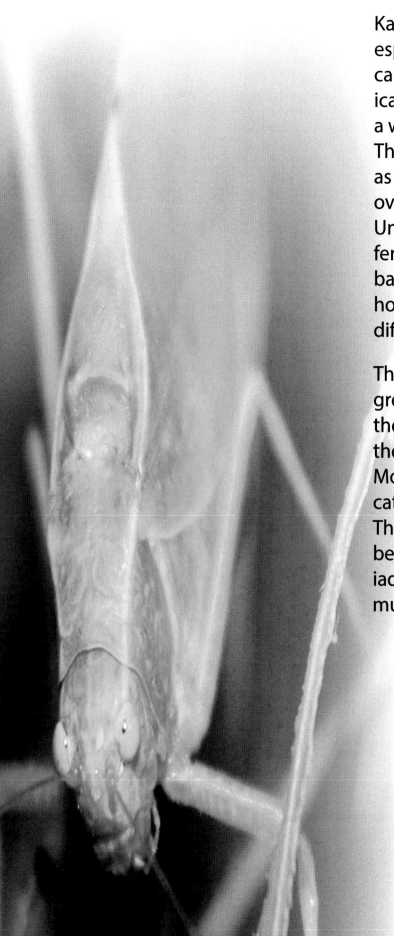

Katydids are actually all around us especially during the summer. They can be primarily seen though in tropical locations due to the necessity for a warmer climate to live and breed in. They do live in drier locations as long as they're warm. The Amazon holds over 2000 species of katydids and the United States is home to about 100 different ones. So if you hear them in the backyard don't think it's just a grasshopper or a cicada, it's a completely different organism.

The locations where they live vary greatly. A lot of them like to live by the water, but they like to also live in the trees and bushes around the area. Most of them blend in with their location to help keep predators away. They can even look like leaves, and because of that they can live in a myriad of locations without drawing too much attention to themselves.

What does a katydid looks like?

The appearance of a katydid is actually pretty interesting. It is usually green in color while others would have pink, gray, tan or brown color. The female katydid is usually bigger than the male katydid. Both male and female katydids have long, strong hind legs which help them with jumping around and moving.

They have four wings that look like leaves. They are very poor flyers though, so you won't be seeing them flying around like other bugs. Some species however have adapted their wings to help them flutter around weakly while they jump which helps them move from place to place easier. Even though they don't really fly nor do nothing more than flutter, some of them have really long wings. In the tropical locations some of them have a wing span of over eight inches long! That's a long wingspan but it's not used which shows the evolution of these critters over the span of time.

The males and females both have tympana, an organ that they used for hearing and are found on their forelegs. The female has an ovipositor, a sword shaped organ found on the end of its abdomen that looks like a stinger that helps them lay eggs.

Can you see the wings of the Katydid? Although it has four wings, the Katydid is a poor flyer.

Here's a closer look at a Katydid. The tympana, the hearing organ of the katydids, are located on its legs.

Why are they called katydid?

The name of the katydid is pretty interesting and many people wonder why they are called as such. Well the origin of the name is actually from the noise the male make when they rub their legs together. If you really try to hear it clearly it actually sounds like "katydid-katydidn't". It's a pretty cool sound and next time you hear a call like that remember that it's a katydid and not a cricket or grasshopper.

The green color of the Katydid blends well with its surrounding, camouflaging the insect and protecting it from its predators.

Their Behavior

Katydids are usually nocturnal which means they are active at night. They make a whole lot of noise in the evenings that's because there are fewer predators at night than during the day. You might hear a few of these during the day, but most of the time you will be seeing these cool insects at night calling for a mate or looking for food.

The katydid prefers to live alone and is not a very social creature. The katydid parents don't take care of their offspring.

What do they eat?

Katydids generally eat leaves and other parts of the plants like flowers. However some of them are predators and can go after small lizards and other bugs.

Katydids like to eat flowers too.

They also eat fruits and dead insects too.

Katydids eat insects smaller than them.

What eats katydids?

The katydids are tasty meals for insect eaters like birds, bats, spiders, snakes, and frogs.

Snakes are one of the predators of the Katydid.

Frogs like to hunt for Katydids also.

How do katydids avoid their predators?

They avoid their predator through camouflage. Their color allows them to blend in with the color of the leaf or of the bark or stem. They can jump quikly that enable them to escape their predators and they prefer to stay on trees and bushes.

Is it a leaf or a Katydid?

Mating and Life Cycles

Katydid mating is pretty interesting and the ensuing life cycles that come about. The katydid actually doesn't live a long time only about a year.

The three stages of development of the Katydid: Egg, Nymph and Adult

Eggs

The katydid would mate during the summer or early fall and the female katydid would lay their eggs using the organ on her abdomen called the ovipositor. The female would deposit it deep on the ground or on plant stems.

The eggs stay in the ground or stems throughout winter and would hatch during spring. The eggs are gray in color, flat and oval in shape and measure about 1/4 inches long.

Female Katydids lay their eggs on plants or in the soil.

Nymph Stage

The baby katydids that emerge from the eggs are called the nymph. The nymph stage is very interesting. They have the adult body, but they don't have wings. At the nymph stage they undergo several molting or the shedding of their hard, outer layer to grow in size. This stage usually last from 60 to 90 days.

Adults

After their final molting, the katydids are now adults. Once they reach adulthood which takes about a few months, they start to reproduce with other katydids and call for other katydids.

They also start to move around with their wings and they can both jump and flutter around to get away. When they get to this stage they don't grow anymore and the process of molting is done. When they reach this stage it's mostly to reproduce and to gather food so they can lay eggs and create another generation.

Katydids are not endangered but they are rare in some cases. In the US there's only 100 different species, and some are not seen as much. They're not close to extinction though and you will still surely see these little critters chirping around in your backyard at night.

Most Katydids live only for a year or less.

An adult Katydid spends most of its time gathering food and reproducing next generations of Katydid.

Disclaimer

The information contained in this ebook is for general information purposes only. The information is provided by the authors and while we endeavor to keep the information up to date and correct, we make no representations or warranties of any kind, express or implied, about the completeness, accuracy, reliability, suitability or availability with respect to the ebook or the information, products, services, or related graphics contained in the ebook for any purpose. Any reliance you place on such information is therefore strictly at your own risk.

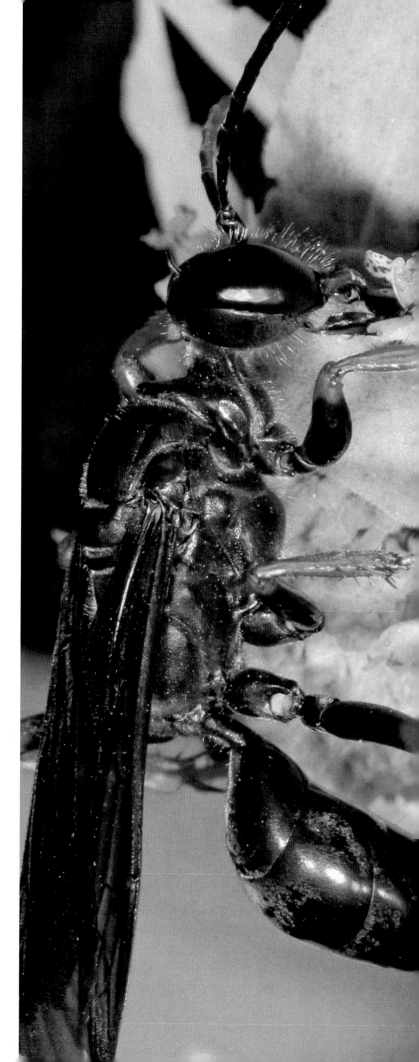

Made in the USA
Las Vegas, NV
14 February 2024